Vulgar Remedies

ANNA JOURNEY

Vulgar Remedies
poems

LOUISIANA STATE UNIVERSITY PRESS)|(BATON ROUGE

Published with the assistance of the Sea Cliff Fund

Published by Louisiana State University Press
Copyright © 2013 by Anna Journey
All rights reserved
Manufactured in the United States of America
First printing

Designer: Michelle A. Neustrom
Typeface: Adobe Garamond Pro
Printer and binder: IBT Global

Library of Congress Cataloging-in-Publication Data

Journey, Anna, 1980–
    [Poems. Selections]
    Vulgar remedies : poems / Anna Journey.
      pages cm
    Includes bibliographical references.
    ISBN 978-0-8071-5219-5 (paper : alk. paper) — ISBN 978-0-8071-5220-1
(pdf) — ISBN 978-0-8071-5221-8 (epub) — ISBN 978-0-8071-5222-5 (mobi)
    I. Title.
    PS3610.O6794V85 2014
    811'.6—dc23

                                                                    2012049696

for David St. John

Contents

FOUR

Why Bioluminescent Shrimp Remind Me of Laura

memoir style [handwritten]

There are lights with a wayward sex
appeal, a weirdness that is   *Randomness* [handwritten]
shrimp cocktail in my steel sink

shot through with miracle.
But that saturated, angelic skin turned
out to be a pink

bacterial slither, a sickness.
There are girls who exist,
like Laura and me, who'd glow—

at fifteen—who'd go up
in flames. We straddled
that concrete median in the donut

shop's parking lot after school
playing the cigarette game:
a lit Camel dropped

between our forearms, a parallel   *Sharing pain* [handwritten]
sting, that burn that made one of us
jerk away first. *Who can stand it*

the longest? Someone lost
each time, although both of us still mirror
the old brands—those flattened

follicles where no hair grows,
those nine white pox
the size of dimes. That night,

I

as we twisted in her cotton
sheets' snakework, Laura said
I didn't know what to do

with a woman's body.
We spooned on her childhood
bed after I flinched   *like cigarette*

from her kiss, turned my spine
to her lips, my face
to the postered wall she'd strung

with dried roses the color of a dark
breakfast tea—those rings
left behind when the heat's

waned and the shapes
settle into the dried
and distant. Husked and

half-healed. I'd trace those forms
with a fingertip: the ovals
of amber I slurred into the oak

grain of her bedside table, the jade
lip of her teacup from which
I sipped, the row of scars on my arm

I now lie about as *chicken pox.* Here,
where I stand at the edge
of my sink with a bowl

of peeled shrimp, where I notice
the sea life still glows after
my lamp sizzles and snaps

the kitchen into blackness. As if a girl
still crouches outside
my window with her wire

cutter and her lucky
skull-lighter. As if I crack the glass an inch
I could smell the smoke.

Vulgar Remedies: Tooth and Salt

After extraction, a tooth is smothered
in salt and burned to stop a wild
animal from finding it. Because if

a fox gnawed it you'd grow a grey
fang and if a bear chewed it you'd wear
its yellow snaggletooth. You've taken me

to the exhibit called *Vulgar Remedies: Belief,*
Knowledge and Hypersymbolic
Cognition in L.A.'s Museum

of Jurassic Technology. We'd married three
weeks earlier on a seaside cliff. *If*
a person doesn't burn

her childhood teeth, I read on the exhibit's
glass case, *she's cursed to search for them*
after death in a pail of blood. Suddenly,

I knew what I should've written
in my wedding vow: how *forever* feels
too vague a word, that I'll stay

beside you until we rise in the shine
of our fangs, our silver pails
filled with blood. We'll recover

all we've lost: our bodies, the blue-slate
roof of our home, each frail and traitorous,
old, unsalted bone.

Leaving Texas

The gold frequencies of cicadas cinch up, then diffuse
their pressed bruises—you hear them throb through the taxi's

cracked windows. So you leave town without the white oak swamp's
humid incense, without its blessing, without telling

anyone. Sunday. You leave without a last banana milkshake with cinnamon,
without the alligator's bleached grin in the antique shop—the skull

you'd saved for. Later, the girl next to you on the airplane nests
a white rat in a red mesh bag in her lap. After

the rattle of takeoff she unzips the rodent and moans,
Lucky's pierced his lip with his own tooth. You didn't think you'd cry

leaving the heat that slept beside you each night, the man
and your shared apartment filled with his instruments, his bows

strung with the hair of horses—their follicled nocturnal
songs. You didn't think you'd sob once but you can't watch the rat's lip

shiver its loose pink eyelet. You excuse yourself,
move through the yellow footlights

to the slim bathroom where the water
in the steel bowl swirls. It's the bluest you've seen in years.

Vulgar Remedies (2): If You Hold a Dying Creature during Childhood

you'll have shaky hands all your life. I thought
caffeine, a strained tendon from typing
with my wrists

curved back. I thought bad
nerves. Instead, it was the bird—a brown cardinal—I scooped

into my shirt from the middle of the street
whose stunned neck rolled
loosely from side to side. I tried not to rock the bird
too hard in my hem. Seven years

old. I walked slowly the whole
way home. My mother helped me pillow
the bird on tissues in a glass hamster
cage. The next day I returned
from school to find no bird. I believed

my mother when she said she drove it
to a special doctor in the country. A week later she told me
she telephoned to find the cardinal
had healed and flown. But since

I've been grown, I've tried to imagine the woman
who lives in the woods and makes
the tiniest neck braces for wild cardinals. I've raised a book

to my face at night and realized my
fingertips shake. And there's a current that curves up
my arm like a broken-necked bird
flying straight to the bone.

Diagnosis: Birds in the Blood

The hummingbird's nervous embroidery
through beach fog by our back

patio's potato vine
reminds me of my mother's southern

drawl from the kitchen: *She's flying,*
flying like a bird! I've heard that

as a child I involuntarily flapped my hands
at my side during moments

of intense concentration. I'd flutter
over a drawing, a doll, a blond hamster

in a shoebox maze. There are ways
to keep from breaking

apart. My guardians. My avian
blood. I believed

birds bubbled inside me—my own
diagnosis—though the doctors called it

something else: a harmless
twitch. A body's

crossed wires. The lost
birds of my childhood

nerves have never
returned. But when you held

my elbow as we walked the four
blocks to the boardwalk,

we saw the brief
dazzle of a black-

chinned hummingbird—the first
I'd ever seen. It sheened

and tried to sip
from my sizzled wrists'

vanilla perfume. I knew
a single one

from the magic
flock had finally found me.

Article for the End Times: Gas-Mask Bra

Elena Bodnar, a Chicago scientist originally from Ukraine,
invented the gas-mask bra.

What makes me claw down
to the lingerie,
what makes me split
another summer
dress's seam: your cigarette
sparked suddenly so my old
panic sweats up again, so I've
spoiled our picnic
under this clammy
stand of Russian olives.
What does it: shock of fireflies
sconcing the pepper vine,
the red buckeye lit like an eye's
riot of veins which thin
at the edge of a gaze, of our
century nuked to a tremble. You
laugh, as I'm now nude
except for the dangle
of one pink embroidered cup
which blows under my left
breast—the other one, pear-
scented, outstretched, an offering.
Let's breathe as the beetles
wing to the wool
blanket their cold
chemical light. Let's kiss
as you daub my nose's tip
with a crushed bug's glow.
You know the rosemary's smoking

in the hills' black socket—
the last rabbit hops by with its
lop ears on fire. As if it got
lit from listening. Let's lean in
until both lobes catch.

Confessions of a Firestarter

Someone arrest me
here in this city park where an ivory

heat combs itself in slow strokes
from the swamp. Where a jogger

and her mallow-jowled
Rottweiler have just

spontaneously combusted—only nipples
of the dog collar's nickel

screwback spikes lie
in the trail's crowsfoot violets. No

vertebrae. No clothes. The newspaper
knows a layer of methane

hangs over the water, ready
to spark. Or maybe it's my dark

night terror that recurs
in which an old alchemist whispers

as she sits on my chest, sizzles
her palms to my shoulders

until my elbows turn
heavy as gold. I don't need a cigarette

to set this trail burning. I don't need
any learned advice:

Leave your man. Run
to another. One thought of you

will char this city. One thought
of that nineteenth-century

hotel with its ivy-drowsed
courtyard of brick where Poe

played as a child, where he whipped
a single chrome wheel

with a violet birch
branch until the stick snapped

between spokes. Where you wrapped your
black belt around my throat

after I asked. I hear sirens.
I hear the twitchy armadillos shiver

from the warp of a near
highway's whine. In the water,

the cypress knees jut
their muscled limbs from the green

ferment, rigor-
mortised, white. Like those women

who kicked a long time before giving up
a finger, a red

dress, a breath, an over-
tongued name. Before each of them

gave her face to the swamp which, as I
pass by, remembering, flames.

TWO

Warning

As heat moves through like its own animal
whose evening pulse is headlights and the reply

of lit cats' eyes. As the amber of Freon
streaked my ceiling and the ceiling

begins to cave, I've had
no AC for days. I've had knuckles

unfold from the oleanders, try to lock
with mine. They're boiled

and hazy in their summer whites—
why I remember

the boy from down the street who often begged
to suck my eyeball. My pupil

rolled under his tongue, the one
whose scent was clove smoke and a soft brie,

winging after a blinding light.
I must've singed the buds

in his tongue to desert thistles—
left a taste like a saint's

charred footprint. As you recede,
memory, a warning: my eye

might make something calcify, a stone
through your sleep, shorn dog

so nude it's another
nocturnal shiver. As sweat

stings my eye, you'll recall the taste,
and the blue cacti,

stoppered with blooms,
will seize like blown crepe.

Dermatographia

Somewhere there's a dress that clings
like a Jackson night, late summer—strapless,

black crepe, a crux where the past
lingers like a Mississippi

vowel drawn out of itself
in my mother, 1963. She drawls,

Hey, Sugar, steps into her date's blue Cadillac.

☙❧

Soon they arrive

at the dance, at the yellow
lantanas corsaging the brick side of the high school.

Pecan, black cypress. Soon her friend Jean

shows up and swings an arm around her nude
shoulders, digs her thumbnail
into her back,

above the black gown's top hem. She's remembered
my mother's skin condition

which causes marks to linger, small scratches
to rise to a red tattoo. On my mother's back

she scrawls the *Z* of *Zorro.*

࿇

Jean from the shotgun house with its fence of wire.

Jean whose mother let the iron linger
too long, seared dark steeples

to her daughter's plaid dresses. Jean whose father
hanged himself in his carpenter's red kerchief after fixing

the back porch's last loose step.

࿇

My mother pulls away as her laugh
snags like crepe. In the school's bathroom

mirror she turns, with her neck
craned to look. She turns, though she can't lose

the letter. She turns
as other girls enter, swinging the door. Her

dark updo licked
by the dimmed lights.

࿇

Dear Zorro,

Where the hell were you, anyway? Masked man,

window-jumper. Where was the getaway horse,
your long sword?

Excuse me, Sugar.
Every woman turns

as if away
from the edge of her own

smoking balcony.

༄

Say my mother now owns not
a single evening gown—not black, not any.

Say the hero was busy
getting a DUI as his Cadillac

burned in a cypress swamp, the mockingbirds

reset to the pitch of metal.
Say this, then,

to the girl in black crepe, to the late
summer fires: there's a sting

that, when it rises, will not quit.

Elegy Where I Initially Refuse to Eat Sand

My mother liked to eat beach glass and sand
people had stepped in. Not many
girls could forgive

such a palate, though I was willing to try
her half-moon-shaped cookies
called Swedish sand tarts

even before I understood the old-world
ingredients couldn't make me cough up
sea shanties or pirates' bones, notes-

in-a-bottle. Like the letter my newly dead
uncle must now sit down to write
since his heart attack slumped him

in the sand near his yellow
house on stilts. He died digging
to heal his hurricane-

split sewer line. I was willing
to forgive his last words to me—
two weeks before—as we swam

through the lukewarm gulf: *Where'd you get
those boobs?* he laughed through
his backstroke. He wore red

seaweed over his bald spot. He refused
dentures, drawled with a lisp that hinted
at what was missing. I was

willing to forgive his last words
because I coughed up a salt wind,
because I hummed, *Way,*

hey, blow the man down! as I kicked the dark
glass: a Budweiser's end. By then the bottle's note
had vanished, or had gotten soaked clear

through. By then I knew *Where'd you get
those boobs?* meant *how violently childhood
bites its mirage into the waves,* or *I painted*

*the beach house yellow after
your favorite storybook bird.* My mother
liked to eat beach glass and sand

people had stepped in. This Christmas I'll ask
for the recipe that will raise
all the gulf's grit in my mouth.

Wedding Night: We Share an Heirloom Tomato on Our Hotel Balcony Overlooking the Ocean in Which Natalie Wood Drowned

for David

We imagine Natalie held a gelatinous green
sliver on her tongue, that its watery

disk caught the lamplight before
she slipped from her yacht

to drown in the waves off this island. This was
thirty years ago. And our tomato's strain

stretches back decades, to an heirloom seed
saved before either of us was born,

before Natalie's elbow
brushed the clouded jade

face of the ancestral fruit
in a Catalina stand, before she handed it

to her husband, saying, *This one.* We hover
near the plate, where the last

half of our shadowed tomato
sits in its skin's deep pleats. I lean

toward you to trace each
salted crease with a thumbnail—

brined and wild as those lines
clawed in the green

side of the yacht's
rubber dinghy. Those lingering

shapes the coroner found—the drowned
actress's scratch marks. That night

we first met, I had another lover
but you didn't/ interesting break

care. My Bellini's peach puree,
our waiter said, had sailed across

the Atlantic, from France. It swirled
as I sipped and sank

to the glass bottom
of my champagne flute. You whispered,

*Guilt is the most
useless emotion.* After Natalie rolled

into the waves, the wet feathers
of her down coat wrapped

their white anchors
at her hips. This was 1981. I turned

a year old that month and somewhere
an heirloom seed

washed up. You felt an odd breeze
knock at your elbow as I took

\

my first step. We hadn't yet met.
Tonight, we watch the wet date palms tip

toward the surf and, curling,
swallow their tongues.

Fable with Prison Nurse and
an Early Morning Embrace

There's a woman who dries Turkish apricots
on her windowsill. This arrangement

and a blue sea knocks
through my aunt's television. But not here,

outside my aunt's wheat-colored doublewide,

where the kudzu is trying to pick
every lock:

red bicycle sloughing
its sickles of rust, the neighbor-girl's blouse

with only one round
pearl button snapped loose. Soon she'll run off,
leave the lean

pin oaks hedging their bets. Before she leaves,
she scatters

a yellow helix of potato

peels for the wild deer. Their white
tails flare in procession,
close as votives. They step as lightly

as my aunt's husband
finally returned

with the white truck, with all their money
he took before

driving all night to Mexico. But that's a dream. It's not
him at five in the morning coming home

to find her awake and slipping
into her prison nurse's pantsuit. When she arrives
at the ward, the men

are mostly asleep, so she has a smoke
as the blue curtains keep

her breath threaded
through the hot, toxic fabric. She might
wait for the sun,

she might wake
one man with the kiss

of a needle and another with the firm

boa-squeeze of the blood pressure meter. She might
hold them each

a little longer, before she lets
go, before the rest of the men know
her neck's

slow tobacco scent, the way she gazes out

the picture window while unstrapping
the machinery,

until the blood
comes rushing back.

Wool Blanket Covered in Nipples

the past needs somewhere to go
—BECKIAN FRITZ GOLDBERG

Its wiry udder slung
over the oak chest at the end

of my parents' bed. Nipples everywhere.
The ones
our first cat sucked up

in grey tufts from the blanket's weave. Weaned
too early, he nursed

from the wool. Dead these
twenty years, he's still here
in the blanket no one will comb out, the blanket

under which the oak chest keeps
safe four pairs of white leather Mary Janes,

faces of the Now Nameless
in old photograph albums: a girl on a fence

in another century. Her rind
of watermelon misses

its center, a bite shows—hole
where the cells were. Her familiar
ears. Glint on her chin. When

did she lose her century? Who knew
her name? When I run

my hand over the wool's tongued-
up snares, I go

somewhere. Though it's

not the same, the underbelly of the Left-
in-the-Room waits

outside time. For a while
I go there, close

my eyes. I click my tongue and begin
to summon them.

The Devil's Apron

refer back to other poem

When my uncle comes back from the dead,
he's hungry. But the plums he left out

before his heart attack
shrivel, like berries
of the red seaweed—their smolder of salt and shattered
mother-of-pearl. He's writing a list

for someone who's had all his teeth
yanked—voluntarily—because *fuck dentists,* he'd hoot, dragging

the pea-green dinghy past his black-eyed Susans
toward the bay's flounder that skimmed the shallows,
quickened like a pulse. His list reads:

more plums, canned salmon, mandarin oranges. He keeps
on: *I can't believe my last words*

to you were, "Where'd you get those boobs!" He's
sheepish and glows

like a grilled sweet onion with one side
charred from a fire.
He asks me to retrieve

his coffee can stuffed with an ounce of Mexican weed
from the garage before my aunt finds it. *This*

being dead, he says, *takes some*
getting used to. He says, *No one's mown the lawn.* Then,
The salt cedars have grown. We sit on the balcony, drop
rotten plums into the surf. *I'll tell you something*

else, he says. *That seaweed the locals call "the devil's apron"*
rises from great depths. It's red to take in all

the violet light. Low tide, its sashes
slip and tangle, like a knot that won't stop
coming undone.

won't
let go of
memory)

Alarm

You sit on the porch swirling
your wine. Red. Tomorrow, there'll be an ache
in each temple and the pillow will row
the scent of a French vineyard further
from your tongue, your night-breath
branched through the batting's
cotton. But not now. Not now,
even though the universe is moving
apart at too many goddamn miles
per second to count. Lately, you've counted
August cicadas dried to the sides of cars,
mailboxes. You found one stilled
in the middle of the sidewalk,
pinched its dry thighs but the shell
wasn't empty and so rang like a house
broken into. Lately, you can set off
an alarm without trying, you can
see yourself stepping out from
the darkened summer porch as if
headed toward anything you could steal.

Black Porcelain French Telephone

Your hoarder aunt took a truckload of angels,
stone frogs, velvet chairs, even the ivory baby
grand piano. You joked: *She'd uproot the front lawn's olive*

and drag it back to Sacramento for the memory. When we
drove up to clean out your mother's house after
her death, you didn't take much: some photographs,

your first pair of eyeglasses, a yearbook. You took
your mother's black porcelain French telephone
from 1922, which sat in its gold-plate handset

on her bedside table. She'd kept the name
of your father a secret until her dementia. Then,
in that space, he was no longer a secret—the past

simply no longer lived there. She'd revised and retold
her story through time: He was the fighter pilot
who proposed then died in Korea. No, he was the stranger

who drugged her highball after the play. Maybe
he was the married director whose picture
you resemble, whose profile she'd folded

into a bookmark, whose face made her voice swoon,
sink low. Although we didn't need another telephone,
you took it. Maybe you want to recover

some trace of the sound—to place your finger
in a hole of the rotary dial so you might finally
reach the right number. One night I found you alone,

your ear cupped to the receiver, the black cord
curled around your knee. I thought you moved your lips
to speak, even though the phone jack was empty.

THREE

One Week before the Vasectomy,
We Stay in the Panama Hotel Bed & Breakfast
in a Room Called Cole's Dollhouse

We'd booked the bordello-themed room's
red sheets, its maroon throw, its three

beaded lampshades amber and glassy
as wounds. We'd slept there before, traced the racy

desk of mahogany—its forties pinup girls
sprawled on old postcards under plexiglass. We'd wrapped

ourselves in velvet. This time, someone's scrawled
the wrong room in the reservation book. Another couple's

there, we learn, all weekend. We take the staircase
to the top floor of the Victorian, open the door

of the room called Cole's Dollhouse. You uncork
a dry white between mint-green walls, between rows

of bisque-head French dolls arranged on shelves
above the bed. They rim the windowsills

in their dim petticoats, sit in a wicker boat across
from the claw-foot tub. Their blondeness quivers

and curls from a lost century: flower girl
with an armful of redbud, one woman whose chest

is a pincushion to her hips, a baby doll's lips
parted as if to speak. I can't

drink enough wine to make their blue
stares stop. Half nude, you sneak into the hallway,

return with extra towels. As I help you drape
the dolls into sleep, my wrist hits a shelf, shakes

a whole row of mohair eyelashes—their bristles
set flapping, the shivered pupils

rattle and skew. The dust, unsettled,
sends its golden

motes through the room and swirls as if
trying to find any form to stick to.

Tooth Fairy Pillow

I'd like to continue
where we left off,
like that light rain in the dogwood, or that voice

swooning after static. In the childhood
house there's a cabinet where the eyes

of potatoes go on
with their deep, mutant reach—dark-
keepers, those tubers

rooted in the gaze. There's a way
back, I know, through the twin bed's

shallow frame. There's a way
back to the life

where my blond nightstand holds

a square pillow trimmed
in eyelet-lace: white

with a yellow plaid pocket
in its center. Before bed I'd tuck a tooth

inside and wake
to find in its place a folded dollar. Let's move on
from right there, and by the way, where

are my teeth? By now
you've snatched a whole set. Tell me,

is that sound
their clacking? I'd like to carry on

the exchange. My trade: six hangnails

for one cry from the childhood
tabby—he'll arrive,

years gone, on the bed, he'll step light
as meringue in his black-
tipped fur. Here's

my final offer: one fistful of red
hair snipped for every afternoon

of sipping
mint tea with my grandfather returned.
My thumb-tip

for a screened porch, that dry wind
through the dahlias. I'll crawl

inside in my whole skin
shrunk down

to the size of a pocket. Let's start again
that burlesque as these potatoes shed eyes

in my sink—blind offering. When I hit

the light switch and climb

the loose stairs toward sleep, I'll listen
for your late-night step, your white

necklace rattle.

And Behold the Locks of the Three Dimensions Are Sprung

—MANDELSTAM

The air conditioning unit invents its dialect: its ticking
gravel-and-shudder. *Should we
buy another one?* I think I might

ask this
each year, but I know
you won't pry

the box from our window—the box that used to cool
your mother's house. You took it home

after her funeral even though it speaks
in obscene volumes through the night. I follow

the rule of insomnia, which is:
think of every possible
beast that could be

hooked to each noise: horse
that kicks from inside

the refrigerator, mother in the metal
AC unit who knocks out

Januaries in a breath. Whole winters
set quivering. Listen,

it's the voice from twenty years ago—growl

of the mountain-troll your mother used to make
as she read to you from *Peer Gynt*
before bed, your eyes slipped

through the crochet's holes. Her larynx
pitched low, almost

cinched to a shudder. Unlikely
lullaby. I

won't ask you to unplug it.

The Spirit of the Hour Visits Big Pappa's Barbecue Joint

No one notices my wings—folded, hollow-
boned. Across the room a girl slurps
red sauce from her fingers, and I fill
with the scent. Its thick molasses
marrows up my carpus, my
metacarpus. This is

why I come here. To remind myself
I was once alive. To weigh myself down,
down to the wishbone that almost
breaks when I remember
how the world tasted—summer rain
on my neck that rolled off,
off like the hour. Or the old house
with its broom closet door—the oak grain
pencil-marked with girl-heights. Once
my sister and I were small enough

to slow down time. We climbed
the cedars on each side of the yard. Scent
peeled from them in strips. Once we
crawled up the swing set's ladders and lay
across its top rungs at dusk. We watched
for long-eared bats, hoped to get bitten
by vampires and changed, until
the flank steak flamed and smoke
moved through the kitchen window,
until the voice

of our mother called us back. The rack
of ribs arrives at my table. I raise

its flesh to my mouth. I'm allowed this
bite before my wing-bones empty,
before I rise, red-lipped, a vinegar
sting in each corner of my mouth.

Nightmare before the Foreclosure

I dreamed the new tenants erased
my childhood. I dreamed they painted

over the broom closet's door. The door
with the pencil marks my parents made each year to show
how much my sister and I had grown. Twenty
years' worth of marks. Yardsticks

on our skulls. We'd balance in the fumes
of the closet's shoe polish, shoulder blades thrown
back. We'd practice
a somber stillness, then flip
and gloat over that year's growth: whole

inches in childhood, a half
inch as we evened out as teens, even a sliver

where we crammed ourselves in when we visited
at Christmas. As we filled the closet with eggnog, with bourbon
as we breathed. I dreamed

the new tenants painted the door. I dreamed each pencil
mark vanished, like rungs of a ladder
tugged out. Where I'm left at the top
unable to climb down. I awoke believing

there'd be no proof left
that my sister and I had ever been
that small. I called

my parents the day after the nightmare. I asked
if they'd bring the door with them
when the house was sold. I asked them

to unhinge it. I asked them
to carry it with them.

Base Notes in Perfume Are Almost Always of Animal Origin

Musk is scrubbing the air of the suburbs—it's like this
each time I return

to my parents' house. The porch lights
drag their wakes. If there's a girl

with black hair in my dream tonight, it's Laura,
who sprays vanilla musk under

the curves of her jaw. Her scent: deer going down,
down to the house in its cool,

sweet weeds to scour the winter
bluegrass for sunflower seeds

that fell from the birdfeeder. If there's a girl
with a white pickup and a pocketknife,

she spreads its blades and pretends
to fan herself as she drives, as she drawls,

Darling. If it's Laura, she won't speak
of the morning she drove me to school,

when we found a roadkill stag—half-dead—
near a curve's blue guardrail. We dragged him

up the bed of her truck to slit his throat,
which took too long to feel

merciful, and made me sick, Laura silent. When she tried
to kiss me later that night after we stole

peat-tongued sips of her dad's Irish whiskey,
I glimpsed the flash of a white tail

in the shine of her iris. I watched it
vanish as she shut off the light.

Mercy

She spends the night with a man who once hunted deer,
who keeps squirrel meat

stacked in his deep freezer, the white ice
rising over red cubes as if the animals'

fur had returned. Cold night, she rolls
closer to fit the curve of his quilt-

slurred spine. She remembers
the patches' outlines: scattered houses snipped

from dead women's linen, those thin
A-frames. Better to snap

the neck of a shot deer than to wait for it
to slowly bleed. He believes this.

A sleepwalker, he often wakes
with a different woman's

head between his knees. He holds
her vertebrae in place as one hand

cups the jugular, the other seizes
the skull. He wakes to the dull warmth

of limbs kicking the sheets, to the scream
of a deer becoming a woman.

Moose Head Mounted on the Wall
of Big Pappa's Barbeque Joint

His form half-disappeared like the hind
legs of your childhood. Like its hooves.
The moose—whose body is now
a stone fireplace with a smoked-
over hole at the heart—stares
elsewhere. One glance at his glass eyes sets
your trigger finger twitching. It's
not a gun snug against your thigh,
just your pulse that holsters
a memory: that boy with the fetish who'd beg
to suck your eyeball. You'd offer
the roll of your right eye, then
the left one's plush. His tongue
tipped with nicotine flicked your veins
a wilder red. You did this, sitting
on the brick wall of the abandoned
bread factory as scattered pigeon spines
vertebraed the mapleleaf viburnum. The flock
once flooded the chain-linked ryegrass
among blue dumpsters, cooing for crusts.
Now the kick of vinegar sours up
from the coral sauce on your rack of ribs,
and you sit with your past's camouflage sliding
off in drops like a season. Like the one
the moose head remembers, which is
why the hunters must've craned his neck
to the right before they stuffed it. A light
snowfall, a starveling ginkgo. So he wouldn't
scare off customers with the snipe
of his stare. So they hung him there,
the rest of him invisible. Who knows
how long he's looked back.

Hide and Seek with Time Machine

The mystery of the childhood
cat who vanished one day in June,

the heat so heavy it left
sand in the front door's keyhole, the clammy mirrors

beaded since the AC
gave out. Gave up

its weather. We searched
the ranch house, the veranda's terracotta

pots, the backyard's monkey grass. We yelled
Pyewacket into the dry azaleas—our half-

brown tabby, half-Maine Coon
with a name so strange people would ask

us to repeat it: *Pyewacket.* My mother
named him after the witch's cat

in a 1950s film. After she downed
two pots of coffee, she tore

the blue cushions from each room's
teak chairs. She shrieked, *Pye!* She finally

yanked back the bathroom's shower curtain
and found our cat who'd stretched

out to drowse in the cool
of our claw-foot tub. I liked to pretend the griffin-

footed porcelain formed a magical animal. One
who'd let me climb in, until we shifted

into one species that prowled the hour
before bedtime. Before night sunk like half the family

photographs in the flood. Before the first house
ticked into its own time zone, now

unreachable by any means. Its blinds
cinched shut, the brass knocker about to lift—

if I remember to bring a breeze—on the red door. Before
the first cat in childhood cools

to a tuft of grey fur in the brass urn
on the mantle. Sometimes I handle its musk,

though it's pulse-less. Sometimes I sleep and think
I feel Pye step lightly up the rungs

of my spine. That's when I return
to coil in the claw-foot tub, to sleep in its

hushed shape, and stay that way
as death drifts by,

calls our names, and remains
unable to find us.

Danse Macabre, Mississippi: My Great-Grandmother Fires a BB Gun

There were black-eyed Susans loose at the hip, the limp magnolia
blooms worked
to a quiver. There were white necks

of her Belgian hens sent cracking. The day Baby Grace died
from strep throat, my great-grandmother

chased her son into their magnolia's
manic tier, fired

lead pellets at the soles of his loafers. That day she laid down
her bouquet-patterned
wedding china in the zucchini patch and stomped.
There were bare

feet in her garden, as her garden grew
gardenia-struck teeth—flung shards. My grandfather's lungs
pulsed like a monarch

on a stone. Later, he will smoke
for fifty years, become a shrink. From the tree

he heard her shelling pistachios—a sound like someone's back teeth
grinding in nightmare. There were pistachios

gone brittle, blue at the lip. His mother,
pacing, craved salt as her daughter

cooled under the quilt. There were faceless Dutch girls
in patterns on the quilt, swallowed in bonnets, each one distant
from the others, as if lost

in so many separate snowfields. There were voids around each one

the shape of the distance between
a boy in the top of a magnolia and his mother's salty

breath over her BB gun. There were tranquilizers so heavy
for years, her tongue

kept thrusting. Grandfather, it must
never have been still.

FOUR

When I Reached into the Stomach
of a Fistulated Dairy Cow: Sixth Grade
Field Trip to Sonny's Dairy Barn

Clover and oats, a tangle of bile-
singed Timothy hay—what Sonny

said we'd feel. Gloves
kissed to our elbows. Ferment of the winter

cow field. I feel a whole
bitten pasture as it broke

down inside her—blue barn
sweet with the atomic

shudder of barley. I reach past
that weave of hot forage to the fuchsia

grove, where after a future
lover and I drop

acid, he'll wrap my neck
and wind my nipples with the fringy mimosas'

burlesque feathers. I reach back
and further through fields

to the French Canadian
with a musket wound blown

through his left side: the stomach wound
that gaped like hibiscus, wouldn't

heal, even as he married
a white-haired girl from Lake Michigan's coast,

fathered two girls. I touch
her cheek, where a platinum

strand splits her eye
from her lip, which opens and shuts

and opens. I watch
her feed him plum halves on a string

so she can pull the desiccated
fruit from his side's portal

to know how matter moves
through his body. Now

the cow's gut contracts and holds
my forearm. I'd scream

except for the throb
of her back's heat, the peat

moss below that pillows
our joined shadow: cow and a girl

grafted as a radical
experiment. No, it's when

I grew a whole heaving
beast for a palm, my wrist which holds

a Holstein's pulse, pull
like a wound where inside the hay

breaks its weave, where the shredded
mimosa won't shut.

Honey Dusk Do Sprawl

—BERRYMAN

When the tulip tree's all damseled out in violet, when I can't pass
a stray window without hungers

in its mirror, I check to see if I'm still
myself. When I'm the girl who daydreams

her own funeral, then asks you about the salivary
habits of ponies, that hissing Shetland,

Princess, muzzles up, grey-lipped,
from your mother's childhood. When her preacher-father

found only the full sink's grimy porcelain, he'd pour the cobalt vase
half full with Jack Daniel's, and a few

dried forsythia rinds plumped
back yellow. He'd weave through the kitchen,

and she'd escape to the barn, until her palms
ran with brown sugar. Tulip tree-wise, honey, we might be

safe for the season. The face of the childhood pony always
torqued for coarse sugar—a bluntness

to the need, like trying to read someone's
lips in a dream. A hiss that rolls

all the way here. Outside, the wind-raved date palms
walk their razors with the sound.

The History in Coffee

Even the house's pulse quickens. Each time
I visit my mother we stay up too late

at the kitchen table, me tracing the oak-knot I once
colored green as a child, sipping a mug's heat. She brews two

pots of coffee a day when I'm away—
three when I visit. Our habit speeds up speech

as it careens off the stove, off our Swedish sand tarts
as they cool in their sugary grit. We laugh and shudder

the straw goat above the fireplace, the brass
urn filled with grey fur from our first cat. I've read

about the Ethiopian shepherd who discovered the effects
of coffee when his goats gnawed the trees'

black beans in the evening, then grew
too wide-eyed and nervy to sleep. They bleated

all night, climbed into trees. My inheritance: an insomniac's
palate—I'll drink even the last, lukewarm sip—the trip

of a heart murmur in which my jittery
valve knocks in hooves or horsefly

wings against a window. My mother and I linger
over the table's stain. The bay window grows dark,

the dark lawn disappears as our doubles emerge
in the glass—our heads and chests severed

by the blinds' walnut slats. We're stuck
clean through, like magicians' women. For now,

we shut the blinds, and our bodies
reassemble. For now, I trace the table's faded

green knot as if its nebula held the whole
past in its fist. As if sped up, we could simmer

and steal from time the pulse of multitudes. We raise
our mugs in the groves of insomnia's

bleat. We keep time under hoof. Our heartbeats rise
as fast as the landscape blackens.

Sonnets to Ambien

Ambien, a sedative-hypnotic drug used by insomniacs,
may cause hallucinations and erratic behavior.

I

A reaper and his phosphorescent lynx
hang from my coat hook. I'm already
this far from sleep. Whole species away.
The pillow swims. Isn't this hot flutter
in each nostril the fur of my nocturnal
angel as she bristles by, and changes
the time zone? The time zone here always
resets to jet lag. As if I fly in each second
from Paris, anew, with my perfumed silks,
my scrawled-on maps. I've tried valerian,
chamomile, lavender, hops. I've eaten
passionflower. Outside my window
the honeysuckle's smothering the summer
locusts. Their cogs and wings grind.

Journal like

2

The snack at three a.m.: buttered cigarettes
in a Chinese noodle bowl. A frieze
of blue mountains along its lip. Sleep's
porcelain borders. Next: a salt sandwich,
a slice of raw bacon. Tell me, bright lynx,
what your grazing pastures grow. I know
the cucumber blooming over brick must hold
the harshest yellows of mid-day, the wide-awake
world. At your central black pond: a circle
of faces from which whispers rise like
scavenger birds. Rasp of grackles as they
love the whites of my eyes like two
rhinestone brooches. They pry them loose,
take off through the screw-pod mesquite.

3

In the country of No Sleep, Not a Doze,
everyone's a distant cousin: the coat hook's
Swedish nose, the lamp's cloisonné orchids
lit between its neck and mine. Even the electric
lynx looks ancestral. Angel, let me tell you
a story: the woman goes out, hypnotized,
into the Denver night. She wears nothing
but a white nightshirt, though it's twenty degrees.
After the car wreck, the cops find her
in the middle of the intersection pissing
the shape of the Land of Insomnia,
which steams as it spreads, which freezes, fixed
to the crosswalk's bars. This country's the largest
island, with one inhabitant, with one light always left on.

There's Another Forest Growing in the Water

from the Swedish folk tale

and uncle, you're there,
where the black-eyed Susans mirror

and meet at the root, lose all
sense of direction. They grow straight

down, down where you warp
and ripple, uncle, down where you lean

on the handle of your blue-
spaded shovel after the hurricane

split your beach house's sewer line—
after the dune grass flooded

and formed its own
wavering lake. After

your death your boardwalk
rotted in the middle, so to get

to the sea I now walk
through the tangle of your yard:

your salt cedars, your string-
bean patch so heavy the whole

fence sways. These days,
there's another forest

growing in the water—seaweed
red as your mustache as it burned

in the funeral home's
oven. What the tide tells me,

uncle: it must've been the first
part of you to catch.

Alarm (2)

Sometimes a woman sets off alarms
with her spine. Like my mother as she walks
through an airport's metal detector—two
steel screws in her back. Sometimes I think
and think past a neighbor's dry cacti
and a sprinkler starts up. I think someone's
roped a scent hound to my hip when I pass
the live oaks on my lawn and the Spanish moss
shivers its silver fox tails. I sail from room
to room in my red hair and trigger
the smoke alarms' sounds. I've found
no cure for the world's reactions. My mother
carries an X-ray in her purse—for proof—
when she flies. I think my dead grandfather
sloughs Irish cells through my scalp. I've
got proof. I've got a mirror that can sleep
through the night, but rises up hungry. I've got
freckles that darken with summer to chart
the route to a sunken city. Its horses
swam off years ago. All the luna moths
in the lampshades drowned. The pile
of stacked cedar someone left has soaked
through—too wet—but as my breath draws
closer, it shifts, and it begins to smoke.

Sonnets to the Egyptian Chamomile Farmers

I

My box of herbal tea promises sleep, human
rights: a fair trade. It promises its third-world
farmers are safe, paid a good wage. The sun-
burnt men tend those apple-scented herbs so I
might finally sleep. Right now, I'm heavy
as blue fields of flowering chamomile.
Right now, I hold the whole dusky outskirts
of Cairo in my mouth. Without honey. Not
a drop. I waft the boiled, grassy taste. I want
my tongue to remember how to rest. Instead
it ticks, begins to whisper: *Habibi,* my
sweetheart, my beloved, my dear.
In my ear, an Egyptian lullaby: *Bee Queen,*
Bee Queen, your keepers are sleeping through time.

2

Would it surprise you to find a white goat
behind each of my teeth? Those blocks
like limestone about to drop. The goats
crushed during construction. Would it
surprise you if a pyramid's rising, right now,
on the back of my tongue, under the red
loop of my uvula that swings like a sun
on a hook? I'd be lying if I said I hadn't
dreamed in corpses' bouquets, the sweet
acacia snuffing its lights, the scent
of a garland in the architecture: woven
mint, wild celery, dill. They make pills
for that, sweetheart. They make tea
from flowers so ghostly they seed on my tongue.

3

Farmer, your fingertips run blue. I knew this,
since I woke with your whorled thumbprints slung
low on my neck—from when you checked
my pulse—slowed to the beat of the dreamworld:
to Almost-Ghost: to the white oak's hole-filled
leaves that drop in slow time. You know,
there's a country in which broken clocks are outlawed. Here,
we're all outlaws. Like in the dream where I can't
see the numbers on my watch and people's lips
stub out words with a blur, as in an overdub. Once,
in my driving dream, the wheel wouldn't stop
spinning, so I tore circles through a forest. An impossible
path. Mornings, I peel my bed sheets from your shape,
find a pile of raked leaves, and they scatter.

Saint Bruise

What I call the small fan of violet
threads under my breasts. I don't know why

my bruise never faded. It's been

years since I was
fifteen and helped Joey Seal

steal the four-foot statue of the Virgin

from St. Mary's Church. Years since
the Virgin's forehead

scarred my sternum to show

how colorfully a girl
can go creeping through a church's

side garden with a boy in leather

who liked to suck eyeballs. Who suggested
we hop the wall and wiggle

the statue from its fishpond, dump

her body in the mulberries by the all-
night bakery whose sign would glow

when the donuts rose hot

from the oven. We dropped
acid until she turned

red in the neon, until the scrape

on my chest—from where
her forehead rested as we carried

the stone—stung

like the memory already
taking root, taking its two licheny

inches in bruise. Once,

as we sat in the fig-
scented bath, another man asked me

what the mark meant, the scar

I touch each night as I stand
near the sliding mirror.

If I comb my wet hair it hangs

just above the flush
of blurred nerves, the old

border, those forked veins: that

door which remains
open for the patron

saint of what breaks, that ghost

of what's always
been broken.

As I Rewind

The hands of the golden-oak clock spin
the wrong way on the wall of my childhood

house as I rewind the Christmas video. It's over
twenty years ago. My young mother's head—

sped up—jerks on the screen. Brunette
in a blue velour day robe. Rewound,

her coffee mug fills a dark inch
each time she sips. The Maine Coon uncurls

from our peach-colored couch, leaps to the window
in reverse. My grandfather's scarred thumb

nudges into view—only once—and I pause
that second. Black shadow: he's behind

the camera. He can't stop
focusing the lens on me. I sit at the green wire

feet of the plastic tree. I smooth shut
the wrapping paper, re-secret the objects, seal

all the ripped seams. The stripes of winter
sun—rewound—run eastward,

and the smoke from my grandfather's cigar
ciphers back into leaves.

Acknowledgments

Grateful acknowledgment is made to the following publications in which these poems first appeared: *The Best American Poetry 2013:* "Wedding Night: We Share an Heirloom Tomato on Our Hotel Balcony Overlooking the Ocean in Which Natalie Wood Drowned" (reprint); *Connotation Press:* "Fable with Prison Nurse and an Early Morning Embrace"; *Copper Nickel:* "Alarm (2)" and "Saint Bruise"; *diode:* "Alarm"; *FIELD:* "Confessions of a Firestarter" and "When I Reached into the Stomach of a Fistulated Dairy Cow: Sixth Grade Field Trip to Sonny's Dairy Barn"; *Hayden's Ferry Review:* "As I Rewind"; *Indiana Review:* "Dermatographia" and "Sonnets to the Egyptian Chamomile Farmers"; *Jabberwock Review:* "Base Notes in Perfume Are Almost Always of Animal Origin" and "Why Bioluminescent Shrimp Remind Me of Laura"; *The Kenyon Review:* "Sonnets to Ambien" and "Warning"; *The Kenyon Review Online:* "Elegy Where I Initially Refuse to Eat Sand," "Mercy," "Moose Head Mounted on the Wall of Big Pappa's Barbecue Joint," and "The Spirit of the Hour Visits Big Pappa's Barbeque Joint"; *The Missouri Review Online:* "The Devil's Apron"; *The Rumpus:* "*Danse Macabre,* Mississippi: My Great-Grandmother Fires a BB Gun"; *The Rumpus Original Poetry Anthology:* "*Danse Macabre,* Mississippi: My Great-Grandmother Fires a BB Gun" (reprint); *Salt Hill:* "And Behold the Locks of the Three Dimensions Are Sprung"; *Shenandoah:* "Honey Dusk Do Sprawl" and "Leaving Texas"; *Southern Indiana Review:* "Nightmare before the Foreclosure"; *The Southern Review:* "Wedding Night: We Share an Heirloom Tomato on Our Hotel Balcony Overlooking the Ocean in Which Natalie Wood Drowned," "Black Porcelain French Telephone," "Vulgar Remedies: Tooth and Salt," and "Vulgar Remedies (2): If You Hold a Dying Creature during Childhood"; *Spillway:* "Diagnosis: Birds in the Blood," "One Week before the Vasectomy, We Stay in the Panama Hotel Bed & Breakfast in a Room Called Cole's Dollhouse," and "Wool Blanket Covered in Nipples"; *Stone Canoe:* "Tooth Fairy Pillow"; *Tar River Poetry:* "Article

for the End Times: Gas-Mask Bra" and "The History in Coffee";
Vinyl Poetry: "There's Another Forest Growing in the Water"; *Verse
Daily:* "Alarm (2)" (reprint) and "Diagnosis: Birds in the Blood"
(reprint).

With profound gratitude to MaryKatherine Callaway, John Easterly,
Jessica Faust, Neal Novak, and all the folks at Louisiana State
University Press.

Special thanks to the National Endowment for the Arts and the
Corporation of Yaddo.